A GIFT FOR

FROM

DATE

A MOTHER'S PRAYER

BY JACK COUNTRYMAN

COUNTRYMAN

A Division of Thomas Nelson Publishers

THOMAS NELSON

Since 1798

NASHVILLE DALLAS MEXICO CITY RIO DE JANEIRO

A Mother's Prayer
© 2014 by Jack Countryman

Published in Nashville, Tennessee, by Thomas Nelson.

Thomas Nelson titles may be purchased in bulk for educational, business, fund-raising, or sales promotional use. For information, please e-mail SpecialMarkets@ThomasNelson.com.

ISBN: 978-0-529-12129-5

Printed in the United States of America

14 15 16 17 18 POL 5 4 3 2 1

www.thomasnelson.com

CONTENTS

GOD'S ABUNDANT MERCY

Rejoice the soul of Your servant,
For to You, O Lord, I lift up my soul.
For You, Lord, are good, and ready to forgive,
And abundant in mercy to all those who
call upon You.

—PSALM 86:4–5

O Father, how wonderful You are. Your love is endless, and Your abundant mercy is new every morning. My heart is filled with praise for Your loving-kindness. Help me as a mother to share Your abundant love with each of my children. May Your Spirit give me the wisdom necessary to guide the precious gifts You have given me. I confess that I cannot live without You in my life. Give me the power of Your presence to live each day for You, my Lord and my Savior. I ask these things in Your most holy name. *Amen.*

A SISTER'S AFFECTION

*Be kindly affectionate to one another
with brotherly love, in honor giving
preference to one another.*

—ROMANS 12:10

Lord, You have said in Your Word to be "kindly affectionate with brotherly love" to those around me. Soften my heart and give me a sensitive spirit to my family as well as those I interact with each day. Let my life be a clear reflection of Your love and care for each of us. Help me, O Lord, to look beyond my own selfish desires that I may see the needs and desires of others. In Jesus' name. *Amen.*

HELP ME NOT TO BE ANXIOUS

*Be anxious for nothing, but in everything by
prayer and supplication, with thanksgiving,
let your requests be made known to God;
and the peace of God, which surpasses all
understanding, will guard your hearts and
minds through Christ Jesus.*

—PHILIPPIANS 4:6–7

Father, so many times I feel myself
worrying about things in my life that
draw me away from You. You have asked me
in Your Word to be anxious for nothing and
I must confess that I need Your strength to
make this happen. Give me a willing heart to
share my life openly with You, holding nothing back. Lord, I thank You for the promise
You have given me. Protect my heart and
mind as I live to serve You. In Your name I
humbly pray. *Amen.*

GOD'S TENDER ASSURANCE

Let us draw near with a true heart in full assurance of faith, having our hearts sprinkled from an evil conscience and our bodies washed with pure water. Let us hold fast the confession of our hope without wavering, for He who promised is faithful.

—HEBREWS 10:22–23

You have invited me, Father, to draw near with full assurance of faith. Thank You for that invitation. Fill me with the power of Your presence that You might forever be the center of my hope. Help me, O Lord, to hold fast to my confession and live a life full of Your love without hesitation or wavering. For I know You are faithful, and I thank You for Your everlasting love. Bless me that I may bless those You have given me to raise and nurture. In Jesus' name. *Amen.*

THE HIDDEN BEAUTY OF THE HEART

*Do not let your adornment be merely
outward—arranging the hair, wearing gold,
or putting on fine apparel—rather let it
be the hidden person of the heart, with the
incorruptible beauty of a gentle and quiet spirit.*

—1 PETER 3:3–4

*L*ord, may the inner beauty that only You can give forever shine through my heart that others may see Your love and grace. Give me a gentle and quiet spirit that glorifies Your presence. Let the beauty of the Holy Spirit shine in my life so that everyone will see how precious and important You are to me. Guard my heart from selfishly living to please others with how I look or what I wear. May I be an example to my children that inner beauty comes from You, and that it is all You see. This I ask in Your precious name. *Amen.*

LORD, HELP ME BELIEVE

"Let not your heart be troubled; you believe in God, believe also in Me. In My Father's house are many mansions; if it were not so, I would have told you. I go to prepare a place for you. And if I go and prepare a place for you, I will come again and receive you to Myself; that where I am, there you may be also."

—JOHN 14:1–3

As I walk through life, Lord, there are so many things that try to draw me away from You, yet You have declared that You are the Way, the Truth, and the Life. Never let me doubt Your love, mercy, and grace, for I yearn to live in Your presence. Let Your Spirit continually direct my path and strengthen my walk. Without You, I can do nothing, but with You, "I can do all things through Christ who strengthens me" (Philippians 4:13). In Jesus' name. *Amen.*

THANK YOU, LORD, FOR YOUR CARE

*Therefore humble yourselves, under the
mighty had of God, that He may exalt you
in due time, casting all your care upon
Him, for He cares for you.*

—1 PETER 5:6–7

Father, I know that You care for me.
Help me to rejoice humbly in the
blessings You have given me as I seek to
know You and the power of Your presence
today. I will empty myself and give You
everything that separates me from You. As a
mother, I need Your tender care to encour-
age and lift me up to be all You wish me to
be. Hold me in Your arms and strengthen
me for Your purpose. I know You have a
plan for me, and I yearn for Your direction.
This I humbly pray in Your name. *Amen.*

GOD'S GIFT—MY CHILDREN

Behold, children are a heritage from the LORD,
The fruit of the womb is a reward.
Like arrows in the hand of a warrior,
So are the children of one's youth.

—PSALM 127:3–4

I praise You, God, for the children You have given me. They truly are a heritage from You. Give me the wisdom to raise each one with the knowledge of a loving Savior. Guide me, O Lord, that my children may know Your saving grace and the power of the resurrection. Protect each one, I pray, and keep them from harm. Give me the wisdom to make the right choices that will glorify You and help them develop solid values for the rest of their lives. And Father, let my life be an example of the unconditional love that only You can give. Praise Your holy name in which I pray. *Amen.*

GOD'S EVERLASTING COMFORT

Blessed be the God and Father of our Lord Jesus
Christ, the Father of mercies and God of all
comfort, who comforts us in all our tribulation,
that we may be able to comfort those who are
in any trouble, with the comfort with which
we ourselves are comforted by God. For as
the sufferings of Christ abound in us, so our
consolation also abounds through Christ.

—2 CORINTHIANS 1:3–5

*L*ord, I need Your comfort every day. You are my strength, and I acknowledge that I am lost without You. Come to me each day and cover me with Your blanket of comfort. You have instructed me to comfort others. Let Your Spirit guide me to accomplish the purpose You have given me and be sensitive to those who need help and the touch of Your love. Through all of this may You be glorified and lifted up. For Jesus' sake. *Amen.*

YOU ARE MY CONFIDENCE

Now this is the confidence that we have in Him,
that if we ask anything according to His will,
He hears us. And if we know that He hears us,
whatever we ask, we know that we have the
petitions that we have asked of Him.

—1 JOHN 5:14–15

You have promised, Lord, that I may come to You with confidence, and You will hear my prayer. Let the confidence of Your promise shine through my life in everything that I do. Let my trust in You speak boldly to those whom You have given me to cherish. Let each day begin with assurance in the power of the resurrection and the forgiveness of sin. For it is only through You that we can have the peace that passes all understanding and the reward of everlasting life. In Your most holy name I pray. *Amen.*

LORD, HELP ME TO BE CONTENT

Now godliness with contentment is great gain. For we brought nothing into this world, and it is certain we can carry nothing out. And having food and clothing, with these we shall be content.

—1 TIMOTHY 6:6–8

Heavenly Father, I realize that true peace and contentment come only from You. Therefore, help me to look beyond the selfish desires that so consume my life. Fill me with the power of Your presence and place within me the desire to be content no matter what my personal circumstances may be so that my reflection of Your glory will shine for everyone else to see. This I ask in Your name. *Amen.*

YOU ARE MY DELIGHT

Delight yourself also in the LORD,
And He shall give you the desires of your heart.
Commit your way to the LORD,
Trust also in Him,
And He shall bring it to pass.

—PSALM 37:4–5

*L*ord, You are the delight of my life, and I thank You for all the things You have given me. Each day, You come to me and fill me with the desires of my heart. You shower me with Your love, and I am forever thankful for the gifts of joy, peace, kindness, gentleness, and self-control. May each of my children see the reflection of Your love in my life daily. I promise to trust in You with all my heart and commit my life to You in every way. Thank You for Your love, mercy, and grace. In Jesus' name. *Amen.*

HELP ME TO BE STRONG AND COURAGEOUS

"Be strong and of good courage, do not fear nor be afraid of them; for the Lord your God, He is the One who goes with you. He will not leave you nor forsake you."

—Deuteronomy 31:6

Lord, You have asked me to "be strong and of good courage," and sometimes I find this very hard. Things in life seem to be more than I can bear. Wrap Your arms around me and hold me close, for I must confess I need the courage that only Your Spirit can give. How wonderful it is to know that You will always go before me, and You will never leave me nor forsake me. Give me the power to live each day in the center of Your presence, and let me sing Your praises forevermore. This I humbly pray in Your name. *Amen.*

ETERNAL LIFE WITH YOU, LORD

*But now having been set free from sin,
and having become slaves of God, you
have your fruit to holiness, and the end,
everlasting life. For the wages of sin is
death, but the gift of God is eternal life in
Christ Jesus our Lord.*

—ROMANS 6:22–23

ather, I want to shout with joy, for through Your generosity and forgiving Spirit, You have given me eternal life. The sacrifice that Jesus Christ paid for my sins on the cross has opened the doors of heaven to welcome me into Your family. Thank You! May I live each day through the power of Your Spirit. Speak to each one in my family that they too may know the power of Your sacrifice. For You are more wonderful than words can say. In Your mighty name I pray. *Amen.*

TO LIVE BY FAITH

Now faith is the substance of things hoped for, the evidence of things not seen. . . . By faith we understand that the worlds were framed by the word of God, so that the things which are seen were not made of things which are visible.

—HEBREWS 11:1, 3

Father, help me to live by faith and not by sight. I recognize that faith is not my wishful thinking but an inward conviction that You will always do what You promise regardless of my circumstances. Through faith, I declare my weakness and at the same time proclaim the absolute trustworthiness of God and Your complete and willing ability to do what I cannot. Help me, Lord, not to have foolish confidence in myself, but to look to You always in every part of my life. I can count on You. Praise God in whose name I pray. *Amen.*

THE FATHER'S FAVOR

"Hear instruction and be wise,
And do not disdain it.
Blessed is the man who listens to me,
Watching daily at my gates,
Waiting at the posts of my doors.
For whoever finds me finds life,
And obtains favor from the LORD."

—PROVERBS 8:33–35

How wonderful it is to know, Father, that I can listen to You through Your Spirit and wait upon Your presence with joy in my heart. For I have found You, and You have given me Your love, grace, mercy, and favor. Let the joy of my heart spill over to my loved ones. Let the sunshine of Your Spirit shine brightly in all that I do. I want to live in the center of Your will each and every day. This I ask in Your most precious name. *Amen.*

THE GIFT OF FORGIVENESS

Bless the LORD, O my soul,
And forget not all His benefits:
Who forgives all your iniquities,
Who heals all your diseases,
Who redeems your life from destruction,
Who crowns you with lovingkindness
and tender mercies.

—PSALM 103:1–4

God, You have forgiven me of my sins, and I thank You. Help me to remember all Your benefits and be thankful for Your loving-kindness. I recognize that You want every part of my life. I want to grow closer to You and know the joy that only You can give. May I always reflect Your Spirit of forgiveness to each of my children. Hold me up with Your righteous right hand that I might not stumble. Let me face everything in life knowing that You will be with me. In Jesus' name. *Amen.*

THE GARDEN OF GRACE

For the LORD God is a sun and shield;
The LORD will give grace and glory;
No good thing will He withhold
From those who walk uprightly.

—PSALM 84:11

Lord, You have promised that You will give grace and glory to anyone who will walk uprightly. Lead me each day as I wander through Your garden of grace that I will always look to You for guidance in every area of my life. It has been said that even a broken tree can bear fruit in the garden of grace. I accept that gift as You freely give me grace every day. Thank You for Your loving-kindness. *Amen.*

LORD, I NEED YOUR GUIDANCE

"However, when He, the Spirit of truth, has come,
He will guide you into all truth; for He will not
speak on His own authority, but whatever He
hears He will speak; and He will tell you things to
come. He will glorify Me, for He will take of what
is Mine and declare it to you."

—John 16:13–14

Father God, You promise that Your Spirit will come to each of us when we accept You as Lord and Savior. You are our Guide in all truth with authority that only comes from Your Word. Guide me, Lord, as a mother to make good decisions for my children and family. Guard my tongue as I interact with friends and those I come in contact with daily. May Your Spirit always go before me. May You be glorified and lifted up. In Your holy name I pray. *Amen.*

EVERYTHING BEGINS
IN THE HEART

*If you confess with your mouth the Lord
Jesus and believe in your heart that God
has raised Him from the dead, you will
be saved. For with the heart one believes
unto righteousness, and with the mouth
confession is made unto salvation.*

—ROMANS 10:9–10

So many times in Your Word, Father, You speak to me about my heart. Please open my heart and fill me with Your Spirit, for You are more precious than silver or gold. You have asked me to trust in You with all my heart and lean not on my own understanding; in all my ways acknowledge You, and You will direct my paths (Proverbs 3:5–6). May these words come alive in my life today as I share the love You have given me with my family and friends. *Amen.*

THE SPIRIT OF TRUTH

"If you love Me, keep My commandments. And I will pray the Father, and He will give you another Helper, that He may abide with you forever—the Spirit of truth, whom the world cannot receive, because it neither sees Him nor knows Him; but you know Him, for He dwells with you and will be in you. I will not leave you orphans; I will come to you."

—JOHN 14:15–18

What a precious gift You have given me—Your Holy Spirit abides within me and will be with me forever. You are the Spirit of Truth who reveals everything to me. O Lord, help me to look to You for wisdom always. I am dependent on the power of Your Spirit to guide my life and bring honor and glory to Your name. Bless me, Lord, that I may in turn bless those You have allowed me to nurture. In Your holy name I pray. *Amen.*

HE IS OUR INTERCESSOR

Likewise the Spirit also helps in our weaknesses. For we do not know what we should pray for as we ought, but the Spirit Himself makes intercession for us with groanings which cannot be uttered. Now He who searches the hearts knows what the mind of the Spirit is, because He makes intercession for the saints according to the will of God.

—ROMANS 8:26–27

Father, You have given the Holy Spirit who continually makes intercession for me at the throne of grace. As with the Holy Spirit, help me to pray continually for each of my children and make intercession on their behalf. I yearn for them to know You and experience Your love. Fill me with Your presence so that my life as a mother will be all that You wish it to be. These things I ask in Your most precious name. *Amen.*

LORD, YOU ARE MY JOY

*"If you keep My commandments, you will abide
in My love, just as I have kept My Father's
commandments and abide in His love. These
things I have spoken to you, that My joy may
remain in you, and that your joy may be full."*

—JOHN 15:10–11

My heavenly Father, I recognize that
my joy comes only from You. Draw
me close to You that I may receive all that
You have planned for my life. I rest in the
power of Your presence and look forward to
sharing with my family Your never-ending
love, mercy, and grace. Help me keep Your
commandments and abide in Your love as I
follow the path that You have chosen for me.
For all of this, I give You thanks. *Amen.*

A HEART OF KINDNESS

Let all bitterness, wrath, anger, clamor,
and evil speaking be put away from you,
with all malice. And be kind to one another,
tenderhearted, forgiving one another, even as
God in Christ forgave you.

—EPHESIANS 4:31–32

*L*et the sunshine of my heart show brightly every day with kindness and gentleness toward each of my loved ones. Lord, help me to walk in love and be an imitator of Your loving Spirit. Give me an attitude of generosity that I might not grieve the Holy Spirit. Let me be a shining example of Your tender love and mercy. You have blessed me in many ways. May the life You have given me be a beacon of light that will glorify Your holy name. It is in Your most precious name I pray. *Amen.*

FULL OF LIGHT

"No one, when he has lit a lamp, puts it in a secret place or under a basket, but on a lampstand, that those who come in may see the light. The lamp of the body is the eye. Therefore, when your eye is good, your whole body also is full of light. But when your eye is bad, your body also is full of darkness. Therefore take heed that the light which is in you is not darkness."

—LUKE 11:33–35

You are the Light of my life. Lord, my heart's desire is for that Light to shine brightly so that others may see the love You have given to me. Cleanse me, O Lord, from any darkness that keeps me from You, for I am lost without Your tender, loving care. Thank You for the guidance of Your Holy Spirit that fills my life each day and renews me to bring honor to Your name in which I pray. *Amen.*

LORD, HELP ME TO LIVE FOR YOU

*But the fruit of the Spirit is love, joy, peace,
longsuffering, kindness, goodness, faithfulness,
gentleness, self-control. Against such there is no
law. And those who are Christ's have crucified the
flesh with its passions and desires. If we live in the
Spirit, let us also walk in the Spirit.*

—GALATIANS 5:22–25

God, You have blessed me with children and a special family. You go before me each day guiding and directing my life with gentleness and loving care. Remove from me anything that does not honor You. May my life be a blessing to those You have given me the opportunity to touch. Help me to radiate Your love with gentleness, self-control, kindness, and faithfulness that I may not only live in the Spirit but also walk in the Spirit. This I pray in Your name. *Amen.*

PRECIOUS LOVE OF GOD

*Love suffers long and is kind; love does not
envy; love does not parade itself, is not puffed
up; does not behave rudely, does not seek its
own, is not provoked, thinks no evil; does not
rejoice in iniquity, but rejoices in the truth;
bears all things, believes all things, hopes all
things, endures all things. Love never fails.*

—1 Corinthians 13:4–8

Father, love is such a precious, tender word that has such great meaning in my life. To know Your love and the sacrifice of Your Son, Jesus, is the greatest love that I can imagine. Each day, You come to me with a love that seeks no reward, but is unconditional and nonjudgmental. You have given me blessings beyond my wildest dreams. Thank You, Father. Let my life share Your love with those who desperately need You. In Jesus' name. *Amen.*

GOD'S TENDER MERCY

But God, who is rich in mercy, because of His great love with which He loved us, even when we were dead in trespasses, made us alive together with Christ (by grace you have been saved), and raised us up together, and made us sit together in the heavenly places in Christ Jesus, that in the ages to come He might show the exceeding riches of His grace in His kindness toward us in Christ Jesus.

—EPHESIANS 2:4–8

*L*ord, through Your tender, loving mercy, You have given me the greatest gift of all—salvation. Through Your goodness, You have chosen to favor me with Your love and life everlasting. Words are not sufficient to express my gratitude for Your loving-kindness. Help me to boast of Your mercy and saving grace that my children will know You and receive You as their personal Savior. I ask all these things in Your precious name. *Amen.*

OBEDIENCE IS YOUR CHOICE

Children, obey your parents in all things,
for this is well pleasing to the Lord ... And
whatever you do, do it heartily, as to the Lord
and not to men, knowing that from the Lord
you will receive the reward of the inheritance;
for you serve the Lord Christ.

—COLOSSIANS 3:20, 23–24

Lord, obedience to You is a choice that I must make in life. I pray that each of my children would first be obedient to You and secondly to me as a mother. Let each step I take glorify Your holy name. Let me walk in wisdom so that others may see Your saving grace. Lord, I know You have given me special work to do for Your glory. Help me to look beyond myself and see what You have planned for my life. May You forever be praised. It is Your most holy name that I pray. *Amen.*

GOD'S PATIENCE NEVER ENDS

My brethren, count it all joy when you fall into various trials, knowing that the testing of your faith produces patience. But let patience have its perfect work, that you may be perfect and complete, lacking nothing.

—JAMES 1:2–4

My Father, I find nothing joyful about the trials You have allowed me to face. They seem to come too often. I realize that You often use trials and suffering to test our faith and help us learn to endure patiently. Give me Your patience with my children that I might be the wise counselor You wish me to be. Lord, You know I need Your wisdom, and You promise to give it liberally merely for the asking. I depend on You—never let me doubt Your love and mercy. In Jesus' name. *Amen.*

THE PEACE OF GOD

Therefore, having been justified by faith, we have peace with God through our Lord Jesus Christ, through whom also we have access by faith into this grace in which we stand, and rejoice in hope of the glory of God.

—ROMANS 5:1–2

Father, I am so thankful that by accepting You as my personal Savior, I have made peace with You. My life has moved from darkness to light, and I praise Your holy name. I confess that we are no longer enemies, for I am Your beloved child. Help me to live in such a way that I might experience the peace of God which passes all understanding. This I humbly pray in Your name. *Amen.*

PRAYER, THE BREATH OF LIFE

"Call to Me, and I will answer you, and show you great and mighty things, which you do not know."

—JEREMIAH 33:3

How thankful I am, Lord, that You invite me to call to You. I recognize that prayer is a vital part of our relationship. I promise to share my innermost thoughts and feelings and to praise and worship You for all that You have done for me. How grateful I am that You have promised to answer me and my requests. I look forward to the great and mighty things that You will show Your servant. I yearn for Your infinite wisdom and understanding so that I might know You and the power of Your resurrection. Praise God in whose name I pray. *Amen.*

LORD, WHAT IS YOUR PURPOSE FOR ME?

Now He who searches the hearts knows what the mind of the Spirit is, because He makes intercession for the saints according to the will of God. And we know that all things work together for good to those who love God, to those who are the called according to His purpose.

—ROMANS 8:27–28

God, there are times when I ask myself, just what is Your purpose for me as I walk through each day? Please search my heart and reveal to me what You wish for me to do to glorify Your holy name. Let Your Spirit guide me as I teach my children to live each day for You. I confess that I cannot do what is necessary alone, but with You, Lord, all things are possible. In Jesus' name. *Amen.*

REJOICE IN THE LORD ALWAYS

Rejoice in the Lord always. Again I will say, rejoice! Let your gentleness be known to all men. The Lord is at hand.

—PHILIPPIANS 4:4–5

Help me to live beyond my circumstances, Lord. I must confess there are times when I do not feel like rejoicing. Fill my heart with Your presence; place within me the desire to rejoice in You no matter what is going on in my life. Give me a gentle spirit that brings honor and glory to Your holy name. You are more wonderful than words can express, and Your unconditional love is sufficient for all my needs. In Your name I pray. *Amen.*

AN INVITATION TO REST IN
THE LORD

"Come to Me, all you who labor and are heavy laden, and I will give you rest. Take My yoke upon you and learn from Me, for I am gentle and lowly in heart, and you will find rest for your souls. For My yoke is easy and My burden is light."

—MATTHEW 11:28–30

*L*ord, I accept Your invitation and come to You with an open heart. I want to rest in Your arms and receive the peace that passes all understanding. Place Your yoke upon me, for I wish to learn everything about You. You are the Light of my life, and I am so thankful that I can always come to You for wisdom, strength, and the quiet rest You have promised. In Your most holy name I pray. *Amen.*

A PROMISE TO BLESS THE RIGHTEOUS

But let all those rejoice who put their trust in You;
Let them ever shout for joy, because You
defend them;
Let those also who love Your name
Be joyful in You.
For You, O LORD, will bless the righteous;
With favor You will surround him as with a shield.

—PSALM 5:11–12

You have promised to bless the righteous, Lord. Place within my heart the willingness to live a righteous life. I need the shield of Your Spirit to surround me as I love and serve my family. I will celebrate Your love and blessings with a pure heart as I live each day to bring honor and glory to Your name. Praise God in whose name I pray. *Amen.*

A HOLY SACRIFICE

I beseech you therefore, brethren, by the mercies of God, that you present your bodies a living sacrifice, holy, acceptable to God, which is your reasonable service. And do not be conformed to this world, but be transformed by the renewing of your mind, that you may prove what is that good and acceptable and perfect will of God.

—ROMANS 12:1–2

Lord, You have asked me to present my body as a living sacrifice, holy, acceptable to You. This I can only do if Your Spirit goes before me and places within my heart the desire to live each moment for You. Let me be transformed by the renewing of my mind to live each day as I bring honor to You. This I ask in Your precious name. *Amen.*

RESTORE MY SOUL

He makes me to lie down in green pastures;
He leads me beside the still waters.
He restores my soul;
He leads me in the paths of righteousness
For His name's sake.
Yea, though I walk through the valley of the
shadow of death,
I will fear no evil;
For You are with me.

—Psalm 23:2–4

Heavenly Father, You are my Shepherd. Each day I look to You to restore my soul and lead me to be righteous, kind, understanding, and a Christian example to others in my life. Your blessings are new every day, and I thank You for Your grace and mercy in my life. Lift me up so that I may praise Your name forevermore. This I humbly pray in Your name. *Amen.*

LORD, YOU ARE MY STRENGTH

God is our refuge and strength,
A very present help in trouble.
Therefore we will not fear,
Even though the earth be removed,
And though the mountains be carried into the
midst of the sea;
Though its waters roar and be troubled,
Though the mountains shake with its swelling.

—PSALM 46:1–3

Father, You are the strength of my life, and in every situation I must face, I know You will be with me. Your Spirit will give me everything I need to solve the many problems I face. Keep me in the center of Your will that I might not lose sight of Your never-ending love. Lift me up that I will always come to You for guidance and strength in my life. For You are my fortress and mighty God in whose name I pray. *Amen.*

HELP MY WALK TO BE WORTHY

*I, therefore, the prisoner of the Lord, beseech
you to walk worthy of the calling with which
you were called, with all lowliness and
gentleness, with longsuffering, bearing with
one another in love, endeavoring to keep the
unity of the Spirit in the bond of peace.*

—EPHESIANS 4:1–3

Lord, help me to walk worthy of the calling You have given me—looking always to You for guidance, reassurance, and strength. May Your love abound in our family, and may we forever have the unity You desire for each of us. May Your Spirit give us the bond of peace that we might show the world Your never-ending love. These things I ask in Your most holy name. *Amen.*